UNDERSTANDING
Your Baby

UNDERSTANDING
Your Baby

Lisa Miller

of

THE TAVISTOCK CLINIC

Series Editor: Elsie Osborne

ROSENDALE PRESS

First published in Great Britain in 1992 by:
Rosendale Press Ltd.
Premier House, 10 Greycoat Place
London SW1P 1SB

Design by Pep Reiff
Production Edward Allhusen
Typeset by Ace Filmsetting Ltd
Printed in the United Kingdom by Redwood Press

British Library Cataloguing in Publication Data
A catalogue record for this book is available from
The British Library

ISBN 1 872803 05 9

The Tavistock Clinic, London, was founded in 1920, in order to meet the needs of people whose lives had been disrupted by the First World War. Today, it is still committed to understanding people's needs though, of course, times and people have changed. Now, as well as working with adults and adolescents, the Tavistock Clinic has a large department for children and families. This offers help to parents who are finding the challenging task of bringing up their children daunting and has, therefore, a wide experience of children of all ages. It is firmly committed to early intervention in the inevitable problems that arise as children grow up, and to the view that if difficulties are caught early enough, parents are the best people to help their children with them.

Professional Staff of the Clinic were, therefore, pleased to be able to contribute to this series of books to describe the ordinary development of children, to help in spotting the growing pains and to provide ways that parents might think about their children's growth.

THE AUTHOR

Lisa Miller worked as a teacher after leaving university at Oxford. She trained as a child psycho-therapist at the Tavistock Clinic, London, where she now works in the Department of Children and Families. Her time is divided between clinical work and teaching; and she is responsible for the Under-Fives Counselling Service which offers up to five interviews for any parent or parent-to-be concerned about a baby or small child.

Her publications include editorship (with Margaret Rustin, Michael Rustin and Judy Shuttleworth) of "Closely observed infants": an account of the method of infant observation pioneered at the Tavistock.

Lisa Miller is married with four children.

CONTENTS

INTRODUCTION

The first year of life is a crucial time. It is only gradually that people have begun to realise that babies need more besides the physical essentials of warmth, food and cleanliness. Of course, babies always must have had attention, fuss, love and worry; but it has taken people a long time to see that things like this are absolutely essential for healthy development. Just as babies cannot grow in body without decent nourishment and cleanliness, so equally they cannot grow in mind – in feelings, intellect, mental and emotional stature – without enough thought and affection being devoted to them.

Obviously, you must know this to be true or you wouldn't be reading this little book. This book tries to focus on the baby's growth in the areas of feeling and thinking and in the corresponding development in the vital capacity for human relationships – the struggle with likes and dislikes, with pleasure and fear, in the context of deepening understanding and growing independence. Parents tend to feel spontaneously that their babies are fascinating and thought-provoking creatures, if at times anxiety-provoking too. This book is meant to chime in with this interest, to help along our natural and necessary urge to understand our babies.

Of course, it isn't just that parents want to understand their babies. Babies have, on their part, a powerful need to be understood. They need parents to receive their communications and to puzzle away at making sense of what happens. It cannot be too strongly stressed that the relationship between babies and parents is mutual. As we shall see in more detail later, the baby is making his or her contribution from the very start. Babies evoke feelings and responses in their parents just as parents do in their babies. It is always a two-way process.

Since each baby is unique, and of course each family, there is no possibility of a book like this giving any sort of precise advice. All it can do is to open up a few possibilities for thinking. Sometimes it is ourselves, our own oddities, strengths or weaknesses as parents that we need to ponder on. Why do we find it so upsetting when a baby does this and take it in our stride when he does that? Why is this so perfectly delightful and that so confusing? How is it that what was right for the first baby isn't right for the second? What sort of things are universally necessary for all babies, and what varies from child to child and family to family?

Finally, as you are working away at understanding your baby, he or she is working away at understanding *you*. Babies are not stupid. On the contrary, they are highly intelligent, persevering creatures. But they are as yet not informed. They do not know anything about the world or about themselves. They have a great deal of learning to do as they travel the wide distance between birth and one year old. From the raw, vulnerable, often rather desperate little scrap who emerges from inside the mother, it is a far cry to the baby who at a year is well on the way to language and independent movement, who is a solid and characterful little person. We never develop as quickly again as in our first year of life.

Just a note in addition: it is difficult to find a way to refer to the baby. Should the baby be called he, she or it? None will satisfy everyone. To call the baby *he* sounds sexist; to call the baby *she* sounds just as neglectful of boys as *he* does of girls; and to call the baby *it* sounds plain rude. In the end, for the sake of clarity, some of the time I call the baby "he" and his carer "she", while fully understanding that not all babies are boys and not all carers are female.

CHAPTER ONE

BEGINNINGS

The nine months inside

It seems a mercy that pregnancy lasts nine months. This gives a woman, or both parents of course, some time to get to grips with the idea that a baby is arriving. For, while pregnancy and the birth of a baby are very ordinary occurrences – after all, reassuringly enough, we were all born – each new baby is unique and so is each pregnancy. This is true in two basic ways. First, the physical experience of pregnancy is different each time. Even in a straightforward healthy pregnancy one baby can seem small and bouncy and the mother can feel sprightly almost to the end: another, perhaps weighing little more, will feel a great dragging weight. Some pregnancies are beset by morning sickness, others (sometimes in the same woman) cause no twinge of this nasty phenomenon at all. Secondly, each pregnancy is different in meaning. The woman who is pregnant at forty after years of trying will have quite different joys and

15

fears to cope with from the twenty-year-old student whose college course is being interrupted. The single mother of a first baby will have different thoughts and plans from the married mother of an already large family. Physical and mental states combine to shape the experience of pregnancy.

Almost all pregnancies involve wrestling with a mixed collection of pains and pleasures. Almost all parents have to try to settle together or within themselves some conflicts. "We want a baby, but do we want it now?" "I thought I wanted a baby but I never thought I should feel so ill." "We're absolutely thrilled but Susan's haunted by worries – she's afraid the baby might be handicapped or something." "My mother-in-law's being terribly difficult." It is rare to find a woman or a couple who do not suffer a whole range of doubts as well as delights.

This is partly due to the circumstances of the pregnancy: was the conception welcome? are there medical problems? but also due to the inescapable fact that everyone has a wealth of ideas and preconceptions about having a baby which all spring into life once a child is conceived. You could say that we prepare to reproduce ourselves right from early childhood. Remember how popular games of mothers and fathers are at nursery. Think how interested small children are in their mother's pregnancies or in small babies. Then all through adolescence and early adulthood most people are quite consciously preoccupied from time to time with the notion of possible children. Our relations with our parents, our brothers and sisters, and of course our partners, past as well as present, all play an influential part in what it means to us to become a parent. We have ideas, conscious and unconscious, about bad and good parenting and about our capacity to perform this major task.

All in all the meaning of having a baby is hopeful and optimistic. On balance most people feel that there is something very important about this central act of creation, as well as something impressive and mysterious. We all hope that the baby will be a little angel and fear somewhere it may be a little demon, but overshadowing the conflict and doubt is triumph, excitement and success. "A new baby is *always* nice", a grandmother of many used to say as a cheerful refrain.

But what does life inside the womb mean to the baby? The mother is gradually getting accustomed to the idea that there is going to be a baby, and the baby is also gradually preparing for life outside. Babies are unquestionably able to survive if they are born at seven months' gestation, and their capacities and reactions are in many ways like a full term child's. So we must presume that for the last weeks of pregnancy babies are capable of being aware of what is happening to them. Research shows for example that they respond to music. Similarly babies hear their mother's voice, not to speak of father's and siblings' voices; indeed, newborn babies often turn to the sound of their mothers speaking as though they recognised the tones. The baby is not only being created physically, but also in every detail of mental and emotional being.

Birth

Let us carry on thinking about the babies' experience. What might birth mean to them? They give up their inside existence, an existence where they are plugged into their mother's system, where they are firmly held and where all their needs are supplied without any sense of want, gap or space. The baby does not know what it is to be a separate person, or what it feels like to be hungry, cold, unsupported or alone. Then the whole of this tight little world starts heaving and after some period, perhaps prolonged, of struggle, the baby is squeezed or catapulted out into a world he or she does not know, where from the first minutes the infant must breathe independently or cease to exist.

So birth is a decisive change for the baby. Indeed, it is one of the great dramas of life. For both mother and child it is quite violent and earth-shattering, and we should not expect to get over it too quickly. On the one hand it is understandable that a mother should want to get back to normal but on the other, "business as usual" can be a misleading motto to follow. Nowadays mothers are up and about as soon as possible, and this is fine so long as they and their families do not let this lull them into denying that something very significant has happened. "Don't give up the dressing- gown too soon", said an older woman visitor to the young mother. Partly she meant, in a cheerful, practical way, that if you *look* perfectly capable and ordinary, people will forget you've just had a baby and expect you to pick up your work as usual. But beneath this lay a recognition: a recognition that the new mother and baby need some time to find their bearings and recover their stability. Outside the school gate the other day two young mothers were chatting: one had a tiny baby in her arms. "Oh, birth is an emotional holocaust, isn't it?" said the other, laughing, but quite sincere.

Most births now take place in hospital. The advantages are obvious. Doctors often strongly advocate a "better safe than sorry" approach, and of course it is a great relief to think that all medical problems will be expertly dealt with. What is important, however, is not to lose any more of the intimacy of a home delivery than can be helped. The reasons why parents who have had a home delivery as well as a hospital one almost always prefer the birth at home are usually linked with the idea that nothing is lost of this intimacy. The drama has stayed a private one and the feelings aroused are kept in the family. Feelings are always stirred up at this time and few women leave the experience of ante-natal care and delivery without a mixed bag of contradictory emotions about the doctors and midwives. Where, as in a home delivery, the parents can get to know the midwife personally, the whole process can be much more friendly than at the other extreme where a woman has random strangers taking care of her at this most vulnerable time.

The presence of the baby's father can be important; it has become standard practice now to raise the question of whether he will be there at the birth or not. To some couples it is essential for the mother to be accompanied and supported by him. Other couples feel differently; everyone has his or her own responses to child-birth which need respecting.

However, if one is undecided it may be worth remembering that fathers who are present at the birth rarely, if ever, seem to regret it.

When the birth really is a difficult or even a dangerous one, it is noteworthy how women vary in their responses. Some seem to be so deeply reassured by the presence of a healthy baby that the bad experience recedes remarkably fast. Others need a good deal of time to assimilate and digest the experience and may want to tell and retell the story, trying to understand what went wrong and what it meant to them before the memory can be laid aside.

From the baby's point of view, it is necessary to make contact with mother as soon as possible. The word "bonding" is often used nowadays when people talk about the essential connection that is made between baby and mother. All future development depends upon the baby's having committed, continuous care from one single caregiver – and of course, in good circumstances this will be the mother. Bonding begins right after birth. It is better understood now in hospitals that her baby should be given to the mother to hold and even to suckle straight away after birth if at all possible. Sometimes we see babies who are so alert and well-focussed that they make purposefully for the nipple at once. The mother of Susanna said, "She seemed to have been well briefed before she arrived!" She described how Susanna looked her in the eye then looked the breast full in the nipple, grasped the nipple in a business-like fashion and began to suck strongly.

But babies differ very greatly. Frances, for instance, was born after a long labour beset with problems. Apart from anything else, she was born full of the drugs which had had to be administered to her mother. Frances continued sleepy, hard to feed, passive and un-hungry for many days before she gradually seemed to work through the effects of the birth and began to perk up and take interest. Simon, on the other hand, was born at home after a brief labour and no drugs at all. And yet the GP visiting next morning looked at him in his crib and said, "Well, he's absolutely zonked, I must say". So he was. Simon took as long to wake up to life as Frances did, but for no readily discernible reason. One cannot help seeing that there are temperamental differences between babies. Each baby's character is presumably being formed before and at birth as it is after – by the events that happen to them reacting with their own particular nature.

Babies vary in their ability to deal with adversity. A good many are resilient and when their needs are met will settle and recover from an unsteady start. The mother of Emma, a third baby, told how upset she felt after Emma's birth not to hold her but to have to watch her feeding waving her arms and legs "on the side" as she put it, while a pleasant but slow young doctor put in stitches. However, Emma's mother was experienced, felt quite clearly that it wasn't the best first hour of life, but had plenty of confidence in being able to make it up to Emma and did so. More striking was the behaviour of Matthew, who was adopted at a week old. His adoptive mother very soon felt that by his attentive and inquiring looks he was conveying a sort of hopefulness and a wish to become attached to her. And attached he very soon became, entirely overcoming an unstable start which might have made a more jittery baby into one difficult to soothe, settle and bond with. For there are babies who are born very sensitive and who need extra help and care. We shall turn to the ongoing needs of the newborn in the next chapter.

To end this short chapter on birth, it seems sensible to add a few words on post-natal weeping. Of course, mothers (and fathers too, not to mention siblings) remain in quite an emotional state for some weeks: we shall think about that later. I am referring to the characteristic fits of sadness and crying that hit mothers a few days after the baby is born. There are several elements to consider here. First of all, no doubt, a mother's hormones are all seething around. Intertwined with this are powerful emotional factors. After the elation of birth and the triumph of producing a new person, and all the excitement of congratulations and delight, there can be a corresponding bump down to earth. So many mothers feel, "Oh, he was so much less trouble when he was inside." The baby outside can be a worry, even when doing well. More fundamentally, the mother has a sense of loss. What was inside is now outside. She, and the baby's father of course, and the whole family – but mostly the mother, has lost a whole way of life as well as gaining a new one. The sense of responsibility, especially if the baby is a first one, is colossal and only gradually gains a proper place in the mother's mind. She often feels lost, small and inadequate and needs a good deal of backing. And even the most experienced mother feels that the first ten days of a baby's life are full of huge ups and downs. One mother of five, watching the midwife write the word "uneventful" against "puerperium" [the ten days after birth] on her record card thought, "Little does she know."

CHAPTER TWO

EARLIEST DAYS

Becoming acquainted

The first three months of a baby's life can be quite tough. I ended the last chapter by saying that the mother often feels lost, small and inadequate. So does the baby. Or at least, we should perhaps be a bit more precise, since the baby can't speak, and say that the baby is quite at sea in a mass of new experiences. There are certain essentials for a baby's development. We know that babies need a central person to look after them. This does not have to be the birth-mother; nor do I mean to imply that nobody else should get a look in – quite the reverse, as we shall see in a minute. But there needs to be someone who for a time will put the baby's wants first on a list of priorities. Of course, we can see at once that this is not at best a one-person job. If you are going to be alert to a baby's needs more-or-less all around the clock, you are probably going to need help, companionship and moral support. And at best the companionship is often the one forged between the father and the mother of the baby.

In one family with a new baby, John, all sorts of ways of helping the mother-baby couple were brought into play. First of all, John's father took a fortnight away from work. This was of primary importance for this particular family. The birth was not an easy one; John was in special care for a couple of days and his mother was quite ill and did not remember nearly as much as she would have liked of the delivery. From the first the father acted as an essential back-up to the mother. He remembered all the details of the birth. He described repeatedly to John's mother what the baby had looked like, what sort of little noises he made, how the sequence of events went, what all the doctors and nurses had said. He shared the anxiety at seeing how squashed up and funny John's face looked, and the intense relief as it became clear that John was a perfect baby.

When they got home the couple felt tremendously proud, with their new baby, new cot, new everything – and yet somehow precarious as though they had not yet grown into their new role as parents. John's mother felt overwhelmed from time to time during this first week. She was struggling away with breast-feeding: should she give extra bottles? how much was John getting? were her nipples getting sore? She felt she might get lost under a rising tide of dirty laundry, and general muddle. At this time the father's presence was crucial as they struggled to find a way of working together. Sometimes father felt as confused as mother, and shared her experience of John as somebody who seemed to be crying before, during and after feeds. Sometimes his attempts to rise above it made him a bit maddening as he prepared bottles with a smile, soothing his wife in what she felt was a superior way. But mostly they seemed to get it right. Essentially, John's father felt sure that John's mother had it in her to do the job properly and he could stand by, help encourage and join in.

This mother also had some useful support from a woman from the British charity, National Childbirth Trust who had a good deal of practical wisdom to offer about breast-feeding. She also called in her friend from down the road who was patient, cheerful and interested, being a mother of several children herself. Later on, after the father had gone back to work, she invited her younger sister to stay, and had her first taste of being the more experienced one, the leader in looking after John.

Many mothers manage with less than this, of course, but it is worth remembering that in all cultures people take into account the need for a new mother and baby – the nursing couple – to have protection and support. In the case of John's mother, she went through a crisis familiar to ordinary Western mothers: the birth seemed to rob her of all sorts of things she had relied upon to give her a sense of identity, and it took some time for a new identity to grow. From being whatever one has been before the pregnancy – a hairdresser, a teacher, a graphic designer, someone who has gained some competence and a niche in society – one is shot into knowing rather little and having to learn by slow steps what it is to be a mother to this baby.

Essential factors:
holding, mopping up and feeding

Looked at in a simplified way, the baby's needs can be reduced to the need to be held and kept warm, the need to be fed and the need to be kept clean. I want to look at each of these physical necessities and to suggest that each of them has a psychological or emotional equivalent.

Holding is the first on the list. No baby can just be laid aside to fend for himself. He has to be picked up and carried: he has to be held to the breast. He has to be kept warm. It is quite clear that babies are frightened of falling and that they need the security of feeling nicely pulled together. Inside the womb they were held from all sides. Now that they are outside they need moulding and shaping. You can often see a baby who has burrowed into the corner of a cot or crib, as though trying to find a home that will give him shape. His earliest experiences of where he begins and ends, of which is him and which not him, start with experiences like that of being enclosed in his mother's arms and offered the breast or the bottle.

The experience of being held and at the same time offered a focus is the first significant one of a baby's life. Babies instinctively tend to go for the nipple, and the nipple or the teat of the bottle acts as a focus to their whole being. Throughout our lives we continue to need this combination of factors: a framework and structure to support us and tasks in front of us to get on with. Here the baby needs to settle to the first version of this. And it is quite hard work, both for the baby and the mother. Just as the baby needs holding in body, so he also needs holding in mind. The eminent English paediatrician and child psychiatrist, D. W. Winnicott, talked about "primary maternal preoccupation". He is talking about the state of mind which a mother needs to be in during the first days and weeks of a baby's life. A mother will have her new baby always in her mind. The baby needs this. He needs to be thought about, puzzled away at, concentrated upon. His mother has to do his thinking for him until he can start to do it for himself. We know from the cases of children who have been deprived of this primary attention that they find it uphill work to make sense of the world around them and to develop into responsive people.

Here is an example of a baby who was having some problems. These problems highlight in a very interesting way some points about a baby's need to be held in body and mind.

Ella's mother sought professional advice when Ella was a few weeks old. Ella was so restless and cried so much that everyone around her had become panic-stricken. She screamed especially at night. She could neither sleep nor let her mother sleep. The screaming had an unnerving quality and it was not only Ella's mother who felt she had never heard anything like it. The doctor had been repeatedly called out and Ella had been thoroughly examined at the hospital, where no physical cause had been discovered. Ella's mother, Betty Dawson, told this tale in a flat and hopeless way. She said that she thought she couldn't cope much longer.

Betty Dawson went on to describe all her present troubles, and quite soon the professional worker involved began to think that she had plenty of reasons for being upset herself. She was a single mother; she had a difficult relationship with her own mother, and her relationship with Ella's father was fraught with pain and distress. The worker listened and began to feel quite overwhelmed by the extent of Betty Dawson's problems.

At the same time the worker observed Ella. Ella lay loosely over her mother's knee. When she cried a little her mother fed her, but Ella did not get down to a good hearty suck. She did not have a feed with a beginning, a middle and an end. Her mother did not hold her firmly and collectedly, but left Ella to hang on to the nipple for dear life. Of course, she was too small to hold on to anything with her hands or to get a purchase with her feet. All her energy went into trying to hold on with her mouth. She frequently slid off the nipple and had to get herself back on.

Betty Dawson finished outlining her troubles. The worker could do no more than comment simply on how angry, depressed and above all preoccupied Betty Dawson must be. Then the discussion turned to Ella and they talked about how distressed and frightened the baby seemed to be. It gave Betty Dawson some relief to think about it in emotional terms – to think about Ella's being bewildered and scared rather than ill. The worker thought that Betty Dawson could be so full of her own very real worries that it was hard for her to think about Ella's. But when Betty Dawson left, accepting the offer of another appointment a week later, the worker was left feeling anxious and depressed herself.

However, when next week arrived Betty Dawson was able to bring the news that Ella had greatly improved, was sleeping and settling far more peacefully. Betty Dawson had thought hard about the conversation she and the worker had had. Then she herself had had an idea that she felt was the key to the whole improvement. In turning things over in her mind she had remembered a remark about babies needing attention. She had then realised that while she fed Ella she had not been looking at her. From this moment she made a deliberate resolve to focus her gaze on the baby while the baby was at the breast. The result was that Ella clearly felt better.

One might say that Ella no longer felt alone with her experiences. She got the feeling of being accompanied by a thinking mind. She felt enclosed and focussed and things started to make more sense to her. Betty Dawson had also taken up the worker's suggestion that babies sometimes like firm holding, and the whole picture of Ella at the breast was becoming a far more comfortable one.

What factors brought about this change? What was the source of Ella's distress, and how was it relieved? Well, of course, pretty well all new babies cry, and some cry a good deal. I shall come back to this again. But the essential point about crying, which I shall repeat, is that it is a communication. Ella was left in the desperate situation of somebody who is broadcasting ever more frantic emergency messages and not having them received. It is as though she were saying, "Help! I'm frightened! Help! Is there anybody out there?" and feeling as though she had no answering call of comfort.

Of course, her mother *was* there. But she was not able really to look at Ella, to think about her, to try to understand what Ella was bothering about. And why not? It seems probable that Betty Dawson was feeling so lonely, so unsupported, so bereft herself that she simply could not look after the baby's feelings. Indeed, she felt utterly bowled over by them. She did not feel like a capable grown-up at all, but more like a frightened small girl left in charge of a job too big for her.

The change came when Betty Dawson felt that somebody attended to *her*. Once she had found not merely a listening ear, but somebody who had emotional sympathy for the plight she was in, she felt understood. Even feeling a little bit understood made her feel better. Then she was in a frame of mind to understand her baby. When she could begin to keep Ella in her mind and ponder over thoughts of her, Betty Dawson came up with a really excellent idea. It was excellent because it turned out to be exactly what Ella needed. It showed that Betty Dawson could be in tune with just what the baby was crying out for.

This example shows several important things. First, nursing mothers need looking after. Second, if the person who is looking after the baby gets too overwhelmed by the baby's distress, that person stops being able to respond to the baby. In the case of Betty Dawson, she felt so let down from all sides that it was just too upsetting to look after the baby until somebody grasped the fact that she, Betty, felt like a needy baby herself. In the case of John, whom I mentioned in the last chapter, father and mother were able to support each other. When one felt alarmed and incompetent, the other could understand that and yet keep in touch with an adult common-sense perspective.

We can also see in the story of Ella something about the intimacy of emotional contact between parent and new baby. New parents need to be in this vulnerable state, highly alert to and influenced by the baby's state of mind. The communication between baby and parent is non-verbal but very powerful. Once Betty was open to Ella's communications, Ella's need to be looked at registered with her mother. Ella couldn't say, "Look at me!" but the message got across nevertheless.

Mopping up

I said earlier that I was going to deal with the basic things about new babies, and cleaning up certainly is one of them. The physical care of the new born is a taxing job. A small baby gets through an awful lot of nappies, needs a bath or a good wash once a day and numberless wipings-up of dribble, tears, runny nose or sick. Laundry is high on the list of jobs. Parents strive valiantly to keep the baby sweet and clean, since nobody is happy with the idea of a dirty, neglected baby.

There are good hygienic reasons for keeping a baby

clean. All sorts of soreness and all manner of infections need to be avoided if the baby is to be comfortable and well. But there are also some interesting psychological factors at work. For the baby, mind and body are very close. Having bodily discomfort or even pain relieved is linked indistinguishably with mental relief.

And the baby needs not only physical mopping up but lots of mental mopping up. By this I mean that just as surely as he evacuates his bladder or his bowels a baby empties himself of unhappiness. A crying baby is conveying his or her messy misery and, like Ella, needs somebody to receive it. Crying, as I said before, is communication. It has meaning. But a baby's crying needs an adult's emotional and mental equipment to sort out what it means.

To return to Ella, who was doing something that all babies do at times. She was trying to get rid of all her primitive panic. In the ordinary way the baby's mother or father is there to soothe the fear. Wiping away tears, offering a feed to take away the pangs of hunger, removing a chilly sodden nappy – all these are practical expressions of care, but they also fulfil powerful emotional needs. The idea that help is at hand, that distress can be shared, is the reverse of being left on your own to cope as best you can. The message is that pain can be eased – mental pain as well as physical.

This is emotionally demanding for the parents. In daily life we have plenty of evidence to suggest that all of us tend to shy away from the raw primitive anxiety of the small baby. For example, think how unbearable people find it to listen to a crying baby in a shop. Luckily, the new mother and father in good enough circumstances are able to set aside time to deal with the baby. And, of course, there is all the satisfaction and happiness that comes from looking after a baby who is on the whole doing well.

It may be that so far in this section readers think I have been putting too much emphasis on the struggles involved. Of course, there are lots of people who coast easily through certain stages in their children's lives. But my impression is that the earliest days and weeks are usually quite a fraught experience, even for the calmest, most well-adjusted and contented people. Also, of course, if everything is plain sailing, you may well not be impelled to turn to this book: you'll be managing without it.

Feeding

Feeding, the third of my essential trio, brings the greatest pleasures when all is going well. It is the central experience of your baby's life. It is the basic experience of taking in and the one on which other sorts of taking in will be based. For babies take in far more than food with their milk. They take in love and knowledge to start with. They grow in mind as well as in body. When you think how vital food is to life itself, in bodily terms, you can also consider how vital the whole experience of feeding is psychologically.

What a lot of feeds a baby has! And how they vary! In this context the baby starts to learn about himself and about other people. In the context of a very intimate relationship (and in the early days an intense one), the baby comes to feel the start of a whole range of emotions. First, there is no doubt but that the new baby feels a need. Rooting for the nipple, settling to suck, brings the earliest experience of a want that is satisfied. But many subtle variations on this theme will emerge.

Consider George, the third boy in a family. At a few weeks old his day full of feeds went like this. About a quarter to six in the morning he woke up slowly and restedly after several good hours' sleep. His crib was by his mother's bed still. She changed him very gently and quietly and fed him while the rest of the house slept. Her breasts were full to bursting and he was empty. He had a large luxurious intimate feed.

However, his next between-meals time was disturbed by his noisy brothers and by having to be put in the pram to take them to school. After they got home he had a filthy dirty nappy and his mother gave him his bath. By the time she had finished, George was really crying. He had got into such a state of being interrupted, kept waiting, hustled a bit that he couldn't settle well to the breast. To begin with he gave it malevolent glares. Then he had a few goes, settled for a while, but didn't take much and fell asleep at the second breast.

However, he had a nice sleep and woke to a different experience again – his mother ready to talk and play as she changed and started to feed him. Then a friend arrived and he was admired and discussed, but the atmosphere of the feeding changed as a third person was included.

Later in the afternoon George got irritable and restless again as his mother got harassed, fetching the boys from school. He had several little snacks at the breast to try to calm and comfort him, but none of them worked terribly well. His mother couldn't give him her full attention and she felt cross and tired. At the end of the day her milk was in much shorter supply. George was handed about. He finally dropped off in his father's arms, but didn't settle well until after his late evening feed when his mother, still tired but feeling comforted and quieter, with the big boys put to bed by their father, could hold him for a long feed which offered more holding than milk.

George had here a whole range of experiences. They were bound together by one constant thing – his mother's presence. In these early days, there is no doubt that the presence and the attention of a steady caregiver is the basis for development. The parents and family feed into the baby more than milk. Their affection, admiration and love actually enter into him and give him the feeling that he is a nice person, a person who inspires love and gives love back. This is tremendously important, though taken for granted and un-remarked in ordinary circumstances. For there will be many times when the baby feels moody and miserable and will need to draw on his reservoir of hope and goodness which is constantly replenished in the feeding situation.

Some questions: Breast or bottle? Demand feeding or routine?

Two feeding questions that loom large in the early weeks are formulated here. What about the first one? Is breast-feeding or bottle-feeding better for baby?

This question, like so many related to the raising of a young baby, cannot be simply and finally answered. The answer is always going to be something like, "Well, it depends." However, it is important to remember that both breast-feeding and bottle-feeding can give a baby a fine, healthy, satisfactory start to life. There is no doubt about that.

The mother's decision, or the parents' decision, is going to depend upon many factors, not the least of those being how the mother feels about feeding a baby. In the early days a lot of mothers feel shaky and unconfident, unsure as to whether they can do it properly. Is the breast milk all right? is there enough? why does baby cry so? Help, support and encouragement are all needed. It certainly is less anxiety-provoking to see the milk going out of the bottle and into the baby. At the same time, there are quite a few mothers who are glad they persevered with breast-feeding and overcame the anxieties of the first two or three weeks. If you are in two minds about it – that is to say, you haven't decided before the baby's birth to bottle-feed – give yourself and the baby a chance. Some babies, as I said earlier, are much easier to feed than others.

But reasonably successful breast-feeding is a wonderful confidence-booster for the new mother. One advantage is that the relationship with the baby is cemented. Nobody but mother can feed him at first. It is convenient and fun to hand him round to be fed, but at first it can be confusing for him. Even if he is bottle-fed it is wiser to let him get to know mainly one person. Plenty of time for variety of acquaintance in a few weeks. These early feeding experiences allow a deep attachment to be formed which is the basis of all subsequent ones.

Demand or routine?

Again, this is a personal question, and the answer varies from family to family. In practice it often seems to happen that at first newborn babies need a lot of allowances made. They need us to adjust to them. During the first six weeks or so most mothers feel that they need to lay aside other burdens as far as they can so that they are available to the baby.

But gradually the nursing couple surfaces to take a place in the larger world. And at some time the baby will need the support and framework of a more patterned day, where night is for sleeping, where there are such things as breakfast, lunch and tea. The fashion for a rigid routine seems to have passed, with parents feeling that it is neither kind nor wise to force a baby to feed exactly by the clock. It seems important, nevertheless, to speak up for flexibility combined with some feeling for order. Otherwise the whole day can go to pot, and the parents and baby alike can start to feel they don't know where they are. Many parents of second children say that number two fitted in quite easily to an existing pattern. But there is no substitute for discovering for yourselves first time round.

All in all, the first weeks are a taxing and exciting voyage of discovery. Your baby is finding out about the world, the outside world – the world of another person, the world of parents' voices, gazes, feeling and smell, the world of milk and mental contact. Your baby is also finding out about himself or herself and an inner world of sensations and feelings – and about how the inner world that is him or her relates to the outer world that is others.

CHAPTER THREE

THE ESTABLISHED BABY

Quite a long time has been spent on the earliest weeks – those weeks which can seem to last an eternity as well as to have passed in a flash. Now we shall turn to the middle months of the first year. First there will be a look at how far a baby has got by three months; then there will follow some sections on the baby from the point of view of mental development along with physical and social progress.

Three months – where are we?

Many parents feel that at three months there is a watershed in their baby's development. As parents, they feel, possibly a bit triumphantly, that they have weathered the turbulent early weeks and come out to rather sunnier waters. The baby is much more of a real person, somehow.

What does this mean from your baby's point of view? The baby's experiences are much more collected. Two very important things have happened. First, by now the baby's whole being is gathered and focused together as we can see by his clear and delighted recognition of those he loves. From the start there are moments of recognition: sometimes a newborn baby turns towards mother's voice as though he recognises it from hearing it while he was inside. But these fleeting events are now organised and mobilised. Baby has a memory. His mind is forming. Just as he no longer has to make an effort to focus his eyes, he no longer has to make an effort to focus his mind. He grasps things both with his hands and with his thought processes. He reaches out deliberately.

The second important thing is that the baby is able to distinguish between things he likes and things he does not like in a far more reliable way. Again, this is a process starting at birth: of course, you could say he has always liked warm milk and disliked stomach ache. But the difference is that now he knows he likes one and dislikes the other. Thinking of his smiles, we can see how they have developed from those breath-catching little preliminary half-smiles which many babies give early in life, through to the point at about three months when he greets his mother or father with a fully developed smile of welcome and pleasure.

As I have implied, we are going to consider developments which begin before three months and carry on beyond – developments, however, which are interesting and easily observed in babies in the mid–months of their first year.

The development of love and trust

From the beginning, our lives challenge us with a mixture of good and bad, pleasant and unpleasant. The foundations of our characters are laid in infancy, and the feeling that we have got it in us to deal with what life has to offer is connected with the repeated good and reassuring experiences of babyhood.

Nobody can have all good experiences. However, in babyhood it does matter whether good experiences outweigh bad. In ordinary upbringing, this does tend to be the case. Parents can be relied upon to come to help a crying baby. Food can be relied upon to take away hunger. The fact that parents don't always hear the baby, or that extra food sometimes makes indigestion worse, are ideas to be assimilated and thought about, given that the baby's preponderant state is one of optimism. Thousands of tiny happenings create the idea of hope and trust. Cold feet are warmed, sore bottoms are creamed, loneliness disappears, fright is appeased. The baby is made to feel better.

Equally, the good feelings – of being a happy baby delighted to see mummy or daddy – are heartily endorsed. His or her passionate attachments (again, the prototype for all subsequent attachments) are requited. Or rather, they are endorsed and requited often enough for the baby to trust in their existence.

Dealing with distress and difficulty

Nobody can be delighted to see their baby every single time; and certainly your baby will not always be delighted to see you. Babies are easily and frequently overwhelmed by a torrent of feelings from within. When George, described a few pages ago, was angry he could not face the breast. He felt it had gone bad on him. A fond grandmother, handed her newest grandson, took one look at his screwed-up face and said, "Oh heavens, dear, I'm not an ogre!" We all retain some of this propensity to see things through rosy or blackish spectacles depending on how we feel about them. But the baby is only just learning how to correct this by checking it against reality, likelihood, memories. So for the time being his granny *is* an ogress, he feels terrified, and he has to be handed back to mum for comfort.

It is hard sometimes to put up with the rage, fear or dislike that comes from an upset baby. However, when parents can keep a good grip on reality and a sense of perspective, they can say something like, "Not too fond of me just now, are you?" and remember that these baby feelings, though violent, are not realistic. The baby does seem to reproach us sometimes, as though we were the cause of his woe, because we are indeed the whole world to him and anything that happens seems to come from us. If we can put up with these baby feelings fairly tolerantly, the baby can have the best chance of growing up not feeling that his nasty feelings are too dangerous to be dealt with.

Nobody, however, can be perfect. Looking on the bright

side, it would be misleading to bring a baby up to think that life can be free of conflict. It is a mistake to think that we can spare babies all pain and upset. In a way, we would love to. It's terribly hard sometimes to feel we can't protect babies from all harsh reality. And, of course, too many harsh knocks will push a baby's development askew. At the same time a parent who rushes in too quickly, trying to spare the baby every particle of frustration or anxiety, is actually depriving the baby of the chance to try out his ability to cope with a little bit of upset himself.

Seeing how much a baby can gradually learn to tolerate is one of the arts of bringing up children. From the start, a baby is learning to be a separate person who will eventually have to draw on his own resources and clear up his own mess. The baby who never has to wait a moment, who is never left alone, isn't given the chance to flex certain important mental and emotional muscles. It's a question of balance, and of adjusting to the particular circumstances of your family and the individual needs of your baby: too much being left to your own devices is plainly not good for you, but never trying out what you can manage isn't good either.

Other difficulties – sleeping and feeding problems – links with the parents' state of mind

There are bound to be questions and discussion between parents about the different aspects of bringing up the baby. That is as it should be. Each individual baby calls forth a way of dealing with him or her which is influenced by their needs and their character as well as by their parents' characters, wishes and ideas and the circumstances of their lives.

People have all sorts of sources of information and help which they use when trying to sort out what to do if baby doesn't sleep or goes off his food, or runs into any of a hundred ups and downs. This book isn't meant to be one which offers you hints and tips, like the practical help which parents get from each other, from grandparents, relatives, friends, Health Visitors and other professionals. It's meant to be a help in thinking about the meaning of what is happening.

If your baby runs into sleeping or feeding problems, major or minor, you will be developing your own repertoire of things to do about it. What we can offer here is the idea that these problems are connected with how the baby is feeling. The baby who can't sleep, wakes up often, is in some way having a problem with being on their own – with letting go and being left, and being left with the world of imagination and dreams. Discomfort, hunger, chilliness, overheating, noise – all these play into a state of mind which will not let the baby rest. Usually warmth, softness, security, perhaps a thumb to suck, are reminders of the good qualities of mother and the other people who look after the baby. But sometimes a persecuted state of mind gets the upper hand. Then the snag is that if this persists for too long, the baby's anxiety gets right under the parents' skin. They begin to worry too. This is inevitable. Indeed, one has to see this worry as a communication: the baby is conveying,

"I am worried." Worrying is a service that one performs for one's children until they can do it for themselves.

However, when sleeping or feeding problems persist, the baby's anxieties can not only provoke parents' anxieties but get mixed up with them. Babies often enjoy a certain degree of protection from family worries: indeed, the mother or father can turn to the baby for relief, seeing hope and life and optimism in him. But when babies do get entangled with their parents' anxieties, they can respond with increasing signs of unease.

A baby girl called Pauline was weaned on to a bottle because her mother's milk was running out. She got a bug with diarrhoea and vomiting; when she recovered, she became terribly "fussy" and started to wake every hour and cry. Now, instead of this being a crisis which her young parents, Mr and Mrs Nichols could weather, things got worse and worse. You might say that it seems understandable that the loss of the breast, the changeover to the bottle plus the nasty infection should combine to shake Pauline's trust in the goodness of things. She needed constant reassurance that her good daddy and mummy were there, and that she hadn't been abandoned to cruel attacks of stomach ache and loneliness. One can imagine that usually a baby would recoup in a few days or weeks, however.

Why did Pauline get increasingly desperate? In this case it turned out to be crucial that Pauline's mother was herself motherless. Mrs Nichols's own mother had died a few years ago when she was in her early teens. So Margaret Nichols had been deprived of all the usual process of a girl growing up: she had neither been able to rebel against nor be supported by her mother. It looks as though the diminishing supply of her milk, Pauline's falling ill, then the sleeplessness, fussiness and crying all came together to shake Margaret Nichols to the core. She began to feel she was a bad mother and that Pauline was a bad baby. Pauline's cries became reproaches. She could neither calm Pauline nor herself. Her young husband couldn't cope with his wife's distress. Fortunately, help was at hand in an old friend of Margaret Nichols's dead mother. Margaret felt impelled to go to her, to talk about her own mother, to grieve and mourn that she wasn't with her. It was as if some of Margaret Nichols's grief and insecurity had gone into Pauline, adding to Pauline's own upset. Margaret Nichols was actually not only grief-stricken but also angry with her dead mother, as though her mother had let her down. When some of these feelings had been touched upon, the storm subsided gradually.

It is surprising how often this happens, though perhaps usually in a smaller or more subdued way. Past events in a parent's life thrust themselves back: memories re-emerge. It is as if when we have babies (especially perhaps the first) we have an urge to re-evaluate past happenings. Certainly what happened to us when we were babies or children or adolescents is very relevant to the kind of parents we are and the strengths we bring to parenting. We can see in Pauline's mother how she couldn't deal with Pauline's feelings of being left alone, let down and abandoned to unhappiness. This is because Pauline's distress reactivated her own unsolved problems. But the episode also brought out Mrs Nichols's strength. She had sufficient good sense and true instinct to turn to the right person – her late mother's friend – and she got the help she needed.

In short, just as parents are sensitive to baby's state of mind, so a baby is sensitive to the parents'.

The development of relationships

I have said earlier that the advent of a baby changes things for everyone in the family. We can see in the example of Pauline's mother how dramatically she was thrown into a state of emotional turbulence: and this is not rare, even in families where there has been no bereavement or other sad event.

In the middle months of the baby's first year everyone is settling down to a slightly new identity. And, from the baby's point of view, all the people in the family are of the greatest interest and importance. It is noticeable how soon babies seem to get a feel of there being a difference between father and mother, that two separate and distinct people are involved. One often hears father saying, "Oh, he always does that when I hold him, but he never seems to do it when his mum does", or something like that. As the first year goes on, we can watch relationships developing rapidly, each with a different quality – mother, father, child-minder, nanny, grandmas, grandpas, brothers and sisters – each person adding something of significance to the baby's knowledge of the world.

I should like to linger for a minute on the significance of

older brothers and sisters. They will certainly have mixed feelings about a newcomer. The important thing maybe is to remember the word "mixed": the elder child who seems impossibly awkward and jealous has also the capacity somewhere to respond with warmth and generosity: equally, the one who is all helpfulness and eagerness harbours somewhere natural and inevitable feelings about being displaced. During the first year, of course, the baby grows up so considerably that matters change quite a bit for the elder child.

For example, Emily, aged three and a half, started off by being the perfect little mother to Sam. She was a bright child, articulate and forward, and she entered enthusiastically into helping mummy. She had thoroughly enjoyed the preparations before Sam was born – the pretty crib, the baby clothes got out and added to, her move to a nice new bedroom. She demonstrated Sam to visitors and modelled herself on her mother. This all worked admirably for as long as Sam (a peaceful baby) slept most of the time. But as he grew and impinged more on Emily's life, she could no longer avoid seeing him as a rival. Her parents noticed that her hugs were getting grimmer. The character of "perfect little mother" began to crack, and it became plain that underneath was Emily, not so much past babyhood herself, unreasonable, upset, outraged at being ousted. Although it can be a headache to deal with sparring siblings, it is probably better in the long run that a child like Emily has all the aspects of her character attended to. It is essential to remember that the good impulses are just as real as the more antagonistic ones. Emily really did want to be a good girl and a big girl. But she also had to grapple with other and more difficult feelings.

Across the road lived Hannah, also aged three and also with a new brother, David. She was quite different. Weepy and clinging during her mother's pregnancy, she seemed convinced that nobody liked her much. She was not always very nice to David. Her parents had to fight against an impulse to scold her and lecture her all the time. David was a demanding baby and Hannah drooped and grizzled, caught cold and refused to occupy herself. However, in contrast to Emily, Hannah began to respond much more positively to David as he grew. It was as though she was reassured by that essential quality in a baby which reassures us all – his capacity to grow and flourish. She seemed to feel that she couldn't have done anything so bad after all with her moaning, jealousy and crossness. David, for his part, showed that interest in and affection for Hannah which nearly all babies demonstrate towards elder siblings. This helped Hannah a lot.

In both these families it was clear that the baby was making his own contribution to the relationship. Sam was a person of hearty and vigorous nature. He had no intention of being treated like a doll. He struggled towards a reciprocal relationship with his sister. Matters might have been different if Sam's tendency had been to be passive and pliable. One would imagine that Emily might have gone on ruling the roost, and that in the end this would neither have been good for her nor for her brother. A baby who is too acquiescent and an elder sibling who is allowed by the baby to be too much the leader does not make a good permanent combination. Emily could have gone on being the little mother and preening herself on her achievements if Sam had been compliant. But then both would have been cheated. Sam would have been deprived of his determination and his individuality. Emily would have also been deprived of necessary self-knowledge. It was painful for her and upsetting for her parents to see how difficult she could be. They had all thought she was so wonderful. But in the end a fruitful relationship with real give-and-take was established. Emily came to like the person Sam really was, rather than the picture of Sam as a sweet little baby. And Sam found Emily fascinating and admired her enormously while still standing up for his rights.

With Hannah and David it was again the sheer interest that David showed in Hannah which proved resilient, and which ultimately made Hannah feel things were probably all right after all. He watched her, smiled at her, copied her as soon as he could. Hannah began to feel stirrings of pride rather than pure rivalry when people said he was a lovely baby. It became gradually clear that her father and mother had room in their minds for two. Both Hannah and David came to realise this, and though their relationship continued rather rivalrous, it had a thread of strong attachment which perhaps would not have developed so well if David had not been the kind of baby who persevered with his attachment to Hannah in the first place.

Babies exert their own force. In a family where the third baby was an adopted one, this was made particularly clear. Mr and Mrs Harriman thought that since theirs was a mixed race marriage they were ideally suited to offer a family to a mixed race child. They had two children of their own, Robert and Jenny, and they adopted Susan, who was six months old. Both Mr and Mrs Harriman loved babies and rather prided themselves on how they handled them. This, plus their experience and Mrs Harriman's profession (she was a paediatric nurse) led them to feel that they would manage the whole business beautifully. However, when Susan arrived, at very short notice, she was a different proposition from Robert and Jenny who had both been fairly easy babies. For instance, they had both by six months been sleeping through the night unless they were ill or upset. Susan was a baby in distress. She had been with her birth mother for some weeks, then with a foster mother to whom she had become attached. So when she was moved yet again, and the whole of her world shifted inexplicably, she fell into a total panic. This panic was broadcast into the family. Mr and Mrs Harriman reacted by experiencing their sort of panic, the content of which was, "Have we made a dreadful mistake?" or, "Is this the right baby?" or "Can we manage?" These thoughts in turn stirred up deeper levels of anxiety, anxieties about not being good enough parents or not being able to tolerate the distress of all their children. For Robert and Jenny became distressed. Robert was five and Jenny three. Robert had been unsettled when Jenny was born. His wish not to have a new baby in the family had been quite strong. Though he had become friends with Jenny, he still had the residual feelings that a baby would push him out, and part of him was prepared to dislike that baby. When Susan cried on and off day and night, ate fitfully, upset his parents, generally behaved like a rather dislikable baby, Robert felt somehow that his nastiness had defeated his generous wishes to welcome a newcomer. He behaved in an angry, guilty, moody way, not wanting to go to school and clinging to his parents for reassurance. Jenny too was frightened. She had expected a sweet tiny baby. She got Susan, who emanated feelings about loss and pain and who was in no frame of mind to smile and make friends. The whole family felt unprepared for this assault.

It was a great help to them all when the parents realised that they were not inadequate: they were under extreme pressure. Here is a clear example of a baby whose distress threw a whole family into confusion. But on a smaller scale it happens often. Once the parents feel they are more or less back in the driving seat then the brothers and sisters can feel that the grown-ups are in charge and that they are able to work out their rivalries and fondnesses within a secure framework.

It is illuminating in this first year to see how the baby watches, listens to and responds to elder brothers and sisters, clearly learning from and about them. These babies are laying the foundation for their own future family relationships, and for their relationships with peers in the world outside the family – with classmates, workmates, fellow team-members, fellow students, colleagues and friends. Just as the bigger children have to contend with a mixed bag of emotions about the new baby, the baby has to do the same in relation to them, learning to find a place in the family whether the first baby or the second or the sixth.

Protection and stimulus

Brothers and sisters, like grandparents or childminders or friends of the family, provide a focus of intense interest for the baby. We are brought to an important question: how do you strike a balance between giving your baby the shelter he needs and providing the sort of stimulus which will encourage an interest in the world?

Very small babies need something of a quiet life, from which they emerge gradually. They are vulnerable, like a snail without a shell, when they first emerge. People instinctively know this and cater to the need for softness, warmth and lack of noise. Fifty years ago babies were left very much to themselves in cot or pram between clock-regulated feeds. Then a reaction set in as parents realised this could be a lonely and unstimulating existence. The pendulum swung quite far the other way, with people realising excitedly what capacity a new baby has for learning and wanting to make the baby's surroundings bright and challenging with vivid colours, pretty mobiles, plenty of action.

At the risk of sounding dull, I would think that here, as with so many things, parents need to strike a balance and to observe carefully what their particular infant needs. William was a third child. His mother was extremely busy with two other small children and a part-time job: she shared a nanny which meant William saw a lot not only of his sisters but of two other children. His mother was both creative and clever with her hands: the place was full of pictures, decorations, toys made by her. She felt that it was never too early to focus and capture a child's interest and her two little girls were imaginative, lively children keen on making things, on painting, writing and singing.

However, the house was noisy and full. William was restless from birth. His mother used to say to the nanny, "He's bored. Bring him in with the others." William certainly glued his eyes to the others. But he continued jumpy and hard to settle, as though he seldom feel soothed and anxiety-free. A visitor saw him one day when he was about two months old. He was lying on the floor on a bright rug. His sisters and the two other children were jumping around, playing a hectic game. The visitor saw William shrink in a rather shocked way as somebody's foot came dreadfully near him. Later they all began picking him up, and before his nanny could say anything one child had shouted, "Boo!" loudly in his ear. This resulted, of course, in wails from William, in recrimination and scolding. Not very peaceful if you have too much of it.

The visitor heard a few weeks later that William was plagued by earaches. Half-seriously she thought to herself, "I'm not surprised, with all that noise going on!". Whatever one feels about that – and of course we must remember that physical and mental come very close together in a baby – it certainly looked as though William might have had too much to contend with and have reacted by becoming unwell. An approach which worked for his sisters needed modifying for him, partly because of all the other children around. Circumstances were different.

William needed more protection, more "babying", less being pushed into the group as though he were already big. A balance had tipped: instead of being alert and fascinated he was starting to get first over-stimulated and then persecuted by the feelings aroused in him.

It seems also as though the child who shouted "Boo!" could have done with a steadying hand. It is really important to protect the baby when he is too small and weak to protect himself. It helps to remember that it does an older child no good to be allowed to frighten a baby with noise, poking or other intrusions. It amounts to bullying in the end, and the poor bully runs up a huge bill of guilt and has to live with a miserably uneasy conscience. Older children, even while we sympathise with their jealousy or impatience, need help in restraining themselves before they do something hurtful.

Babies need to feel reasonably safe, safe in the feeling that they are in their parents' minds, safe in the routines which build up in their particular family, safe within a structure of what they come to know and to expect. From this base they can stretch out to new experiences. It is comforting to remember that they have within them a natural impulse to growth. It isn't *all* up to us. We provide setting and objects of attention, but our babies reach out of their own accord.

Emerging into the world

I have just said that babies reach out of their own accord, and indeed this is literally the first step in play that many of them take. Babies of three months or so reaching for a teething ring or a bit of blanket, grasping it, bringing it to their face, eyes and mouth, examining it, sucking it, are taking a step in understanding that there are things out there which are not themselves. In play a baby seeks to find ways of thinking about the world around in order to grasp its meaning and to understand it.

Responsiveness and sensitivity

Right from the start, a baby is attracted by sounds, sensations and sights. It seems as though a bright light, or something else clear and definite to look at, provides a focus not only for the baby's physical eyes, but for his mind's eye. Small babies gazing at their mobiles are not only having their visual senses pleased but they are also feeling more "together" as their mental processes are focussed. Thought begins. A mobile of apples and pears tinkling in the breeze is giving rise to ideas: what is movement? what is redness, yellowness, shininess?

The first object of this interest and attraction are people; the mother and those who feed and care for the baby, the people whose faces and bodies – not to speak of voices, actions and minds – the baby comes to know. People continue to be the main source of interest for the healthy baby, but interest spreads out fast. The mother of a baby boy, Ralph, had no doubt but that Ralph loved his feeds. She had the impression of someone who concentrated intensely, who worked away at sucking and who yet had enormous pleasure from many of his feeds. He would lie on her knee after the feed was over, mouthing and smiling. One day she saw something that took her attention. She went up to his pram. Ralph did not see her. He was looking intently up into the thick green leaves of a tree which overshadowed the pram. And he was making sucking movements with his mouth. It was as though he had something of the same experience from looking up at the green sunlit tree as he did at the breast. On another occasion she saw him do the same – attending and sucking – when his aunt played the piano. From many little examples like this we can see how responsive babies are to sensuous experiences that capture their attention and indeed move them deeply. The appreciation of beauty exists in babyhood.

Memory and thought

This story about Ralph thinking over his feeds and recapturing similar lovely feelings from seeing and hearing the tree and the music tells us something about the development of memory. The baby develops a mind which retains ideas. To begin with, we have to act as a baby's memory, and indeed we have to think for him, or perhaps *with* him. When he cries and we soothe him, in the knowledge that although he is angry or scared, there really isn't anything too dreadful wrong, the baby has the experience of being in touch with a mind which has a different perspective from his own. It understands what his mind did not understand. It remembers what he did not.

Countless experiences of mental contact enable a baby's mind to grow. The point at which thinking can really be said to start is probably the point at which a baby is able to call things to mind when they are not actually there. To begin with, a baby is dependent on the mother or somebody else actually being there. But when the baby can call her to mind in her absence, remember what it is like to be comforted (for instance) he or she is starting to draw on their own mental resources. A baby girl, Anna, was seen starting to whimper in her cot. Then a thought seemed to strike her. She looked at her thumb, and put it in her mouth. She clearly remembered that this had helped her last time.

We talk about babies "taking things in". I said earlier that they take in much more than milk when they feed. Amongst other things they take in the experience of being thought about, and this is an essential ingredient in their learning to think.

Play and communication

Play is not only to do with a baby's learning about the world out there. It is to do with taking in new experiences, but it is also to do with feelings and ideas. Thus it is also about the world inside the baby; the world of their wishes (what they would *like* to happen), the world of their fears (what they are *afraid* might happen), the world of their developing imagination and intellect.

Ralph, sitting on the floor at seven or eight months, was clearly preoccupied with his set of plastic cups. He would put things in them. He would also put things in his mouth. He would take them out again. His mood of concentration showed that he was grappling with the ideas of inside and outside, how one thing can be contained in another, how you get that thing out when it's in. Before babies have words they have concepts, and the development of language has a history that extends far back in a child's life.

The baby is pushed on from within by powerful unconscious pressures to make sense of what happens to him. Ralph had had by six months many experiences intimately connected with inside and out, the sorts of experiences that have been discussed earlier in this book. The breast goes into his mouth and comes out. Milk goes in but doesn't come out. Things come out of his bottom end. Tears come out of his eyes and roars out of his mouth. But his mother and father hold him safely, and his cot holds him too. His mind has started to hold on to things, but sometimes these things slip out. The earliest physical experiences which were pretty well indistinguishable from mental ones are starting to get separated out. He starts to think about sameness and difference.

Ralph also seemed to be wondering how things work, or how things happen. After he finished feeding he lay back and scrutinised the nipple of his mother's breast. Then he earnestly took the nipple between his forefinger and thumb and then, (said his mother to a friend with a giggle) "he tried to unscrew it!" On one level that was a joke: Ralph knew nothing yet of tools and construction. But his mother had an intuitive feel that he had had the sort of thought which would grow later into an enquiry about how things are made and how they work.

Ralph was plainly also taken with the idea of how things connect. In these middle months babies make a start on getting the idea of a gap between themselves and other people or other things. I have talked about the unconscious communications with others which a baby makes from the start. But gradually he develops the capacity to communicate deliberately as well.

The development of language is intimately linked with the development of a child's understanding that he is a separate person. Communication through action, play or words, crosses a gap – the gap between two people.

To begin with, we as adults are the ones who understand that there is a gap to be crossed. We understand the need for babies to develop their powers of communication: we see that we must communicate through action and through words from the start. As I said earlier, many new babies turn towards their mother's voice as though they had heard it before – which indeed they have, except that they were inside her then. The voice thus starts as a familiar sound. The sound soothes and envelops a baby and is part of his sense of being held by what he knows. It soon comes to be connected with comfort, or with awakening his attention, conveying love, affection, the wish to understand.

Most parents instinctively talk to their babies, right from the early days. From the very simple, "Mmm, nice, nice", or "Poor old thing, poor old thing", our language helps to give shape and meaning to what is happening. We do not feel it is silly to talk at a more complicated level than a baby can fully understand. We move ahead of the baby, who is eagerly trying to catch up, and we beckon to him. Many of us give long commentaries on what's happening, especially if we're alone with the baby: "Who's a nice girl then, a really nice girl . . . We're going to have a bath, mummy's got the bath here. Let's get hold of you; what about the nappy then . . . golly hold on . . . just a mo . . . mummy's coming back, we want the tissues."

This is not to suggest that there is no place for peace and quiet. That would be quite wrong. But babies need to be lent words and to have their experiences formulated for them in language some of the time.

Of course, soon they start to "talk" back. Again, parents and the other older people in a baby's life use their imaginations, their judgment and their hunches to try to grasp what a baby means and to translate it both into appropriate action and into words. Sometimes the message is clear. When Jane, sitting on the floor, lifted both arms and looked beseechingly at her mother, her mother said, "Oh, you want to be picked up, do you?" and suited the action to the words. Thousands of little interchanges like this keep the baby's interest in communication alive and vigorous. It is satisfying to experience a want, have it understood and attended to, satisfying to communicate successfully.

Not only wants are attended to through language. Fears and distress are greatly helped by being put into words. A long process begins in babyhood and carries on through childhood; the process of giving vague but frightening anxieties a name and understanding them. Nameless worries, unthinkable and unspeakable, are the stuff of nightmares. It is surprising how early children can respond to being talked to, and how some of the meaning seems to seep through to them before they have words of their own. If you think your baby understands, she probably does. Be sceptical of people who tell you she doesn't.

Moving on: mixed feeding and teething

Fashions vary in relation to the introduction of mixed feeding. Twenty-five years ago there was a passion for giving babies little tastes of things from a few weeks or even a few days old. Fifty years ago many babies tasted nothing but the odd rusk, some juice and cod liver oil, till they were nine months. It seems plain that the limits are wide: certainly both of these options seem to have resulted in satisfactory grown-ups!

The central fact is that whenever you give bits of this or that, a baby's basic diet needs to be milk for quite some time. When people overdo the solid food at the expense of plenty of milk sucked from breast or bottle, it often seems to be related to some hint of worry about the baby's dependent state. A young mother whose baby was bottle-fed used to be secretly haunted by a wish that the baby would grow up soon, because she was worried that there might somehow or other be a dried milk shortage. She felt silly about this, telling herself that only a huge catastrophe could produce such a thing, and anyway surely there would always be cows? But the fear still popped up in her mind. One might guess that this fear was linked to her own milk supply's having given out, but the point here is that she found it quite hard to carry on being aware that the baby was very dependent still.

Your baby needs to have the kind of feeds he had as a small baby gradually phased out. An incidental advantage of breast-feeding is that the baby is guaranteed time to be held close, time to suck, time for bodily intimacy and its linked psychological intimacy. With the bottle the baby often learns to hold it himself. This is fine as long as not too much closeness is sacrificed too soon.

Nature gives us a hint about solid food. Most babies get their first teeth around the middle of their first year. The impulse to chew takes over from the impulse to suck. We might think what it means to a baby to acquire hard gums, sharp teeth, and the wish to sink them into something. Teeth can be tools; they can be weapons. The wish to bite can be linked with vigorous seizing and digesting, or it can be linked with attacking and hostility.

Certainly teething seems to be a time of anxiety for a lot of babies. Sore gums may be associated with the baby's growing up and feeling much more aware that he is cross and wants to attack something. A mother took her baby to the doctor, saying he wasn't well; he was teething. "Teething produces nothing but teeth!" she was told. But she went away unconvinced. She was sure that teething had made her baby feel unwell. We can remember again that in babies physical feelings are close to – sometimes inseparable from – mental ones. Colds, rashes, slight fevers can be expressions of mental states at the same time as expressions of bodily upset.

Back to work:
the mother who returns to her job

Before we move on from the middle months we ought to

consider that a large number of women who go back to work outside the home do so during this period of a baby's life. You cannot be helped much by a little book like this over the question of whether or not to do so. In each individual case there will be a number of powerful influences at work: the financial situation of the family; the ideas that the parent or parents have about the kind of life they want their family to lead; the sort of investment that the mother and the father have in their careers. Everyone will want to work out the best arrangements for child care that can possibly be managed. All sorts of factors need considering. For instance, it does not take much imagination to see that a baby needs to get to know a fresh person gradually if possible. In order to work things out well it is desirable that we should, as parents, be able to put ourselves in the baby's place and think what he needs, feel a little of what he feels.

This can tax our emotional resources. There is a temptation to think that the baby won't notice too much and won't miss mum. While there is no doubt but that in good circumstances a baby copes with it, there is also no doubt but that they *will* notice. The mother who for one reason or another opts for returning to work also opts for some degree of stress. There are compensations, of course, but it may not be possible to make your return to work entirely anxiety-free for either you or the baby. It is much better, however, to be able to see that your baby is sometimes cross, anxious or fratchety, and for him to feel that you understand this, than to push away the idea that his mum's return to work has any meaning for him.

CHAPTER FOUR

GROWING TOWARDS INDEPENDENCE

I am now going to consider the last three months or so of baby's first year. There are no sharp divisions in development, and the sort of things we shall be noticing do not happen suddenly. Much of what I shall say has links with what I have already said. However, there are dramatic developments in the second half of the first year. Your baby moves away from you. They crawl, and are weaned. Some babies crawl early and some late; the time of weaning from breast or bottle varies. But these individual variations do not alter the general fact that your baby by a year old has a separate existence from you of a different kind from the earlier separate existence.

Comings and goings

From the start of life babies are learning about beginnings, middles and ends. They need a satisfactory proportion of feeds which follow a meaningful shape: they want their food; they know they want it; it comes; they need it badly at first, then less badly as hunger is satisfied, and the feed comes to an end. Then they are left to digest it, to realise something has finished, and to think it over. Finished, till another one comes. This is one important example. They also get used to their family members disappearing and reappearing, for anything from a couple of minutes to hours or days at a time. They often play games with toys where things are thrown away and have to be got back for them. It is no accident that "Peep-O!" and "Where's so-and-so?" are beloved by older babies. These games give the baby food for thought. Things can be invisible, yet not cease to exist. You may be afraid something won't come back – but look! it does come.

Crawling away

Learning to crawl makes a great deal of difference to a baby's life, just as it makes things very different for a mother or father when they have a mobile baby. Being able to move at their own wish and of their own accord must mean a good deal in terms of a baby's feeling of independence. Of course, it will have different meanings at different times. Sometimes a baby will be crawling out, full of cheerful confidence, to see what's happening somewhere else. Sometimes the baby will be driven by anxiety to crawl after mother, dreading letting her out of sight. Sometimes the crawling will be away from something the baby doesn't like. On the one hand, your baby will have more freedom; on the other, more attention may be needed than in the days of more stationary behaviour.

Weaning

All the early gaps, breaks and absences are practice runs for weaning. Of course, babies are weaned from the breast on to the bottle, or from the bottle on to the cup, at different times. Toddlers often cart bottles around for a long time. But there is a sense in which all these different patterns can mask the fact that at eight, nine, ten months the baby is definitely saying goodbye to the life of the suckling, the life of the baby-in-arms or the baby on the lap. He will never be a little baby again.

When a baby is being weaned from the breast at about this age, it is often possible to see how he has a variety of emotions about this loss. Some babies wean themselves quickly, unable to stand a long-drawn-out goodbye. Some are hard to wean (and I shall return to this). Some bite the breast crossly, some are clearly sad and mournful, some have tummy upsets or colds.

Thomas was a thriving, cheerful baby who had fed well at the breast. From the time he was six months his mother worked part-time. This, combined with all sorts of other signs of growing up including a mixed diet he enjoyed, ushered in his weaning at nearly ten months. For a few weeks before he was finally weaned Thomas was rather quiet. He had a couple of colds. He was tetchy on and off. His last feed came and went.

A family friend saw him one day sitting on the floor by the dishwasher with his nose running. He was dismally extracting spoons and forks and putting them languidly into his mouth. He seemed to be acting a little play about chilly, empty, uncomfortable things in his mouth. By way of welcome, he passed the grown-up a nasty wet floor cloth and looked at her. She wondered if Thomas was communicating something about how he felt – as if a wet blanket of gloom was clouding his spirits.

Some weeks later Thomas was again on the kitchen floor when the same friend came in. But this time he turned to her with a radiant smile. With happy noises he indicated that he was playing with a shiny copper pan with a little water in it. He splashed it slightly and chortled. He had recovered his spirits.

The watching adult felt that Thomas had rediscovered in himself some of the lovely feelings he used to have when he was at the breast. Unfriendly spoons and a soggy cloth had been replaced by the sparkling pan and the fun of playing in water. From being miserable, runny-nosed, full of spiky cold feelings, Thomas had moved back to feeling interested, focussed, held again. He had discovered he could feel like this without the help of the breast-feeding relationship. His good baby experiences were past for ever, but new versions were appearing.

Thomas looked older. His communications were not only energetic but more mature. Talking was obviously round the corner. Weaning accomplished is a spur to development. By this I mean that there are tremendous gains to be made in saying goodbye to some stage which is outgrown.

The struggle to grow up: wanting what you can't have

Throughout life we are saying goodbye to the stage we have just left. Goodbye to babyhood is the first of the series. There is always a mixture of conflicting feelings in us about changing and developing and moving on. Babies are by no means exempt from this. To put it simply, one aspect of a baby's character will be all for pushing ahead to new experiences. In the same baby a contrary impulse will be pulling back, nervous of change, afraid of losing the well-loved and well-known, not wanting the pain of loss.

Again, we need to look for a balance. There is such a thing as a baby who is almost too ready to behave as though she were independent. Helen was an early crawler and walker, hot foot in imitation of her elder sister. She was always clambering, sometimes dangerously. She tried to feed herself and succeeded, and she held her own bottle early on. Her parents were rather proud of her. However, it seems as though Helen had been overdoing it, and in her baby way feeling positively all-powerful, as though she could do absolutely anything. She started to come a cropper, both literally and otherwise. She began to fall over. She had a long series of disturbed nights, during which she wanted to be held and hugged and nursed. Her parents instinctively realised that she needed to stop acting as if she were two or three, and to allow the vulnerable side of herself to have attention.

But there are babies who are quite the opposite and need extra thought and help in order to let go of established ways. We often see this at weaning. In the ordinary way, most mothers take a good part of the responsibility of the weaning process on themselves. They decide to cut out a late feed, or to introduce a mixed lunch; babies respond and contribute by being more or less co-operative or by actually showing that they need either more or less than they are being offered. In most cases this runs smoothly and the end is reached by a sort of mutual agreement, but with the mother in charge. However, some babies are distinctly harder to wean than others are.

If you have a baby who is like this then you may be called upon to devote time and thought to it. The whole idea of wanting something you can't have, of wishing something would happen that won't, is one that all babies must grapple with. Indeed, we never cease to do so. Numberless little incidents give a baby practice in the art of learning to say no to himself. These incidents are manageable. They are also important because a baby's tendency is to feel that his hopes or wishes actually are very powerful. That is to say, he feels his wish for a feed brings the feed magically. He learns life is more complicated than that, that other people have lives and minds of their own, and that life sometimes says no to you of its own accord.

At weaning time life says to the baby, his mother and

family, "No, you can't go on being a baby for ever. Even if you do go on sucking at the breast or having bottles, you're *still* not going to be a baby. Nothing can stop the passage of time and the process of growing up." A baby who clings to breast feeding is just as much in two minds about it as one who gives it up in a mood of sweet reasonableness. It's just that the side that wants to cling on is temporarily winning. There is also the side which wants to grow up, to gain independence, to let mother go away in a spirit of trust and generosity. This side needs backing. It is there somewhere. Often when there have been prolonged negotiations between mother and baby over weaning, there is a sense of relief all round when it is accomplished.

Losing a small baby, and gaining a small child

It can be hard to distinguish between a baby like Helen who needed to go back a few steps and to be babied all over again and a child who needs help in separating out and saying goodbye. One of the factors which adds to the complexity is the fact that not only the baby is giving up breast feeding, his mother is too. And though the situation may be less noticeable in a bottle-fed baby, there are still feelings about losing a little baby and gaining a little child which affect the mother and the whole family.

To attend first to the way in which weaning from the breast can be a loss for the baby's mother; this is a goodbye for her too. Often both mother and baby wordlessly acknowledge that the breast has had its day and put it aside without real trouble. The baby has plenty of feelings about it, but the feelings don't get out of control because the mother is not overwhelmed.

Where the mother does get overwhelmed, it is frequently because she has not only the baby's feelings to deal with but also some difficult feelings of her own. These feelings may make it seem impossible not to give way to the baby's wishes. A whole range of arguments can be produced by a mother who half feels the time is ripe for weaning, but half cannot face it. Perhaps she argues that it seems so cruel – the milk's there, the baby wants it: why shouldn't he have it? Perhaps she points to the long suckling period in different cultures, cultures where economic necessity makes protracted breast feeding common. Yet she knows that her baby does not need the breast for its nourishment. She feels more that he needs the comfort, the sucking. In a case like this, to wean or not to wean has become an issue.

Maybe it is that the mother needs some backing and help, as she tries to steel herself to put up with distress from her baby. Both mother and baby have got into the way of bowing in front of a threat. The threat isn't put into words, but it is lurking around nevertheless. This veiled threat says that if the breast is taken away, the baby's distress will be unmanageable. The unspoken theory is that weaning is a catastrophe, not a natural end. The baby believes this; the mother believes this. It is as though the baby has come to feel he will not survive without the breast, and his mother is not in a state to feel cheerfully convinced (or even sadly convinced) that this is just his imagination. His mother behaves as though she agrees with him; and perhaps a part of her *does* agree, and feel that she too will be unable to survive the parting. The adult side of the mother needs backing. In the best circumstances the backing comes from the baby's father, who can help both mother and baby.

Conclusion

At the end of the first year, your baby is ready to look at the world in a new way. Whatever the pattern of existence before, there has been a sense in which a feeding relationship – that is to say, a twosome – has been central. Many people may have been significant in his or her life. But the baby has always needed to be somewhat attached to somebody older. This remains so, but what is developing is a sense of being a separate person, and a sense that other people have relationships not just with him or her but with each other. In a two-parent family we can observe this growing interest in the link between father and mother. In a one-parent family the baby will still be observant of and fascinated by mother's relationship with other adults.

In short, the reign as baby is at an end. Whenever the next baby comes along – in a few months, a few years, or never – there is still a sense in which the lap is now free. It is available for a successor.

FURTHER READING

The Making and Breaking of Affectional Bonds, John Bowlby, Tavistock Publications, London, 1979

Through the Night, Dilys Daws, London Free Association Books, 1989

Thinking about Parents and Young Children, Martha Harris, Clunie Press, 1975

The Diary of a Baby, Daniel Stern, New York Basic Books, 1990

The Child, the Family and the Outside World, D. W. Winnicott, Penguin Books, 1964

HELPFUL ORGANISATIONS

The Tavistock Clinic, The Tavistock Centre, 120 Belsize Lane, London NW3 5BA, London offers the following national helplines:

    Under-Fives Counselling Service (Tel 071 435 7111)

Also, in conjunction with the Child Psychotherapy Trust:

    CRY-sis (Tel 071 404 5011)

    Parentline (Tel 0268 757 077)

    The Association for Post Natal Illness (Tel 071 386 0868)

Organisation for Parents Under Stress (OPUS), 106 Godstone Road, Whyteleaf, Surrey CR3 0EB (Tel 081 645 0469)

Parents Anonymous London, 6–9 Manor Gardens NN7 6LA (Tel 071 263 8918)

National Childbirth Trust, Alexandra House, Oldham Terrace, London W3 (Tel 081 992 8637)

Gingerbread Association for One Parent Families, 35 Wellington Street, London WC2 (Tel 071 240 0953)

UNDERSTANDING YOUR CHILD

ORDER FORM FOR TITLES IN THIS SERIES

Send to: Rosendale Press Ltd, Premier House,
10 Greycoat Place, London SW1P 1SB

Price per volume: £4.75 inc post & packing

Understanding Your Baby by Lisa Miller . . . . . copies

Understanding Your 1 Year Old by Deborah Steiner . . . . . copies

Understanding Your 2 Year Old by Susan Reid . . . . . copies

Understanding Your 3 Year Old by Judith Trowell . . . . . copies

Understanding Your 4 Year Old by Lisa Miller . . . . . copies

Understanding Your 5 Year Old by Lesley Holditch . . . . . copies

Further titles in this series in preparation from: Understanding Your 6 Year Old to Understanding Your Teenager

Total amount enclosed: £. . . . .

Name . . . .

Address . . . .

. . . . Post code . . . .